Flawsome

A
JOURNAL
TO
EMBRACE
YOUR
LOVABLE
INNER
WEIRDO

Delia Taylor

CASTLE POINT BOOKS
NEW YORK

www.castlepointbooks.com

The Castle Point Books trademark is owned by Castle Point Publishing, LLC.
Castle Point books are published and distributed by St. Martin's Publishing Group.

ISBN 978-1-250-28726-7 (trade paperback)

Cover and interior design by Melissa Gerber.
Images used under license by Shutterstock.com.
Editorial by Monica Sweeney.

Our books may be purchased in bulk for promotional, educational, or
business use. Please contact your local bookseller or the Macmillan
Corporate and Premium Sales Department at 1-800-221-7945, extension
5442, or by email at MacmillanSpecialMarkets@macmillan.com.

First Edition: 2023

10 9 8 7 6 5 4 3 2 1

THIS BOOK BELONGS TO

_____

IT'S NEVER FELT BETTER TO BE
FLAWSOME

WEIRDOS, UNITE ! Let those inner quirks be front and center, shine your strange sparkles, and be proud of the oddities that make you, *you*. When flawless facades show up at every turn—from advertisements and film to social media—that valley between reality and perfection gets harder to cross. But perfection is meaningless. All those flaws you're told to fix are actually just added detail, brushstrokes on your very own work of art that make you a masterpiece. Change your mindset from flaws to flourishes and revel in the artistry of what it means to be spectacularly individual.

On the pages of this journal, you'll find quirky inspirations and guided prompts to let you leave your uncertainties behind and celebrate your eccentricities. Jot down your thoughts page-by-page or skip around, depending on the topic that speaks to you in the moment. Get jazzed up and enjoy those happy tingles that come with feeling totally yourself, know your fellow flawsomes appreciate you, and embrace all the qualities that make you extraordinary.

Power up your awesomeness and celebrate what it means to be FLAWSOME!

Julie:

You have a lot of flaws, but you're also kind of awesome.

Charlie:

SO I'M FLAWSOME?

–Love in the Villa

Flaws + Awesome
= Flawsome

Heck yeah, what a combo. Make a list of some of the areas that you think make you a lil' different than the average person. If any of these feel like "flaws," why do they feel that way? Circle the characteristics that make you feel most awesome.

_____

_____

_____

_____

_____

_____

_____

_____

_____

_____

_____

_____

I PRIDE
MYSELF
ON BEING
TRAGICALLY
UNCOOL.

—Kate McKinnon

Basic Math

If you're not cool, you're hot. Yessss. Whether it's being the one who bumps into everything because you're taking it all in, the one with no filter because you're unapologetically authentic, or the one with a drawer full of perfectly pristine Pokémon cards that emphasize your organizational skills, there are endless ways in which "uncoolness" is actually pretty freakin' hot.

WHAT'S YOUR FAVORITE AWESOME QUIRK? WHY?

_____

_____

_____

_____

_____

_____

_____

_____

_____

_____

_____

If you feel like a weirdo, it's okay because weirdos rule the world.

—Aubrey Plaza

Friends Among Us

_____

_____

_____

_____

WHAT ABOUT THEM SINGS TO YOU?

_____

_____

_____

_____

_____

_____

_____

_____

_____

_____

I WENT TO COLLEGE
FOR MUSICAL THEATER,
WHICH MEANS I'M
WHAT'S KNOWN AS
A TRIPLE THREAT.
THREAT #1: I CAN ACT.
THREAT #2: I CAN SING.
AND THREAT #3:
I'M ANNOOOOOYING.

—Gianmarco Soresi

Pew! Pew! Pew!

Watch out for the triple threat, friendos. If you had to name your trifecta of goofy and great powers, what would they be?

_____

_____

_____

_____

_____

_____

_____

_____

_____

_____

_____

_____

_____

_____

MY HEART IS
FULL OF GOLD
VEINS, INSTEAD
OF CRACKS.

—Leah Rider

Embrace that Golden Joinery

Treat those marks on your heart like *kintsugi*, the Japanese art of mending what's broken with gold.

WHAT'S ONE THING THAT MADE YOU FEEL LIKE YOU WERE FALLING APART IN A WAY YOU DIDN'T EXPECT?

_____

_____

_____

_____

_____

WHAT UNEXPECTED GOLDEN LESSONS CAME FROM COBBLING YOURSELF BACK TOGETHER?

_____

_____

_____

_____

_____

I always wanted to be somebody, but now I realize I should have been more specific.

—Lily Tomlin

Ta-Daaaa!

Way to make an entrance. What are some qualities about yourself that you might not have asked for but make you exactly who you are? When have those quirks made you stand out in a way you liked?

_____

_____

_____

_____

_____

_____

_____

_____

_____

_____

_____

_____

_____

_____

_____

I AM SO CLEVER THAT SOMETIMES I DON'T UNDERSTAND A SINGLE WORD OF WHAT I AM SAYING.

—Oscar Wilde, *The Happy Prince and Other Stories*

It's All Greek to Me

Or pig Latin. When have you caught yourself effusing some serious nonsense (or an authentic but overly dressed word salad) and you just ran with it? What does it feel like to let yourself speak first and think later?

_____

_____

_____

_____

_____

_____

_____

_____

BLAH, BLAH, BLAH, BLAH

_____

_____

_____

People say nothing is impossible, but I do nothing every day.

Take It Easy, Champ

You might be the type who brings that all-star energy every day or the type who feels forced to ransack your internal cabinets to find extra batteries more often than you'd like. In either scenario, embrace the nothingness. What is it about sitting still and recharging that is hard for you, and what about it feels like that sweet, sweet relief?

THERE'S NO ROOM FOR DEMONS
WHEN YOU'RE SELF-POSSESSED.

-Carrie Fisher

Oujia Look at That

Get in touch with your inner light. How would you describe your spirit?

_____

_____

_____

_____

_____

_____

_____

_____

_____

_____

_____

_____

_____

_____

_____

Sometimes you lie in bed at night and you don't have a single thing to worry about. That always worries me!

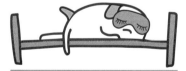

–Charlie Brown

Overthinking Overtime

What are the weirdest things you worry about or have worried about? Do you ever wonder if honey made by killer bees is poisonous? How do those thoughts make you unique? What helps you saunter past those worries and return to being your marvelous self?

_____

_____

_____

_____

_____

_____

_____

_____

_____

_____

_____

KLUTZINESS IS ENDEARING.
i LIKE IMPERFECTION.

-Elizabeth Banks

Falling for Yourself

So long as it doesn't send you careening off a cliff, lean into your clumsiness. What kind of awkward tendencies—be they physical, verbal, or nonverbal—do you have that show others you're human? In what universe might they be seen as strengths?

_____

_____

_____

_____

_____

_____

_____

_____

_____

_____

_____

Would I rather be feared or loved? Easy. Both.
I want people to be afraid of how much they love me.

—Michael Scott, *The Office*

Take Me to Your Leader

Do you feel like you're running the show, or do you feel like you're following someone else's lead? Neither is bad: the world needs both! What do you like about this position? How would you like others to treat you?

_____

_____

_____

_____

_____

_____

_____

_____

_____

_____

_____

_____

I HAVE A LOT OF
GROWING UP TO DO.
I REALIZED THAT
THE OTHER DAY
INSIDE MY FORT.

-Zach Galifianakis

Play Time

It's not childish—it's called not being dead inside. How can you divvy up the different facets of your personality so you can be responsible and reasonable when it matters and playful and childlike other times? What fun things give you that *huzzah* feeling?

_____

_____

_____

_____

_____

_____

_____

_____

_____

_____

_____

_____

_____

_____

_____

I didn't like the idea of being foolish, but I learned pretty soon that it was essential to fail and be foolish.

–Daniel Day-Lewis

Fool's Errand

What exercises in failure have you performed for yourself or for a much wider, much more public audience? What about failing fantastically was a worthwhile endeavor?

_____

_____

_____

_____

_____

_____

_____

_____

_____

_____

_____

_____

_____

BOOOO!

GO HOME!

CRINGE!

PEOPLE WASTE THEIR TIME
PONDERING WHETHER A
GLASS IS HALF EMPTY OR
HALF FULL. ME, I JUST DRINK
WHATEVER'S IN THE GLASS.

—Sophia Petrillo, *The Golden Girls*

Cheers!

Drink up from your life cup. When you stop to calculate the meaning of everything, you can miss the moment. What keeps you from diving into new experiences headfirst?

_____

_____

_____

_____

_____

_____

WHAT GOOD COULD REMOVING JUDGMENT DO FOR YOU?

_____

_____

_____

_____

_____

_____

_____

Why don't I just step out and slip into something a little more spectacular?

—Liberace

Make a
Spectacle

Be extra today. Take a risk and don that sparkly thing. Go full goth girl. Roll around in puffy paint—whatever! What spectacular gambles can you take that will make you feel like you stand out from the crowd?

_____

_____

_____

_____

_____

_____

_____

_____

_____

_____

_____

YOU ARE BLIND
TO REALITY
AND FOR THAT
I AM MOST
PROUD.

—Moira Rose, *Schitt's Creek*

Put On Those Blinders!

Not everything has to be based in reality. What illusions of grandeur make your life better? What suspension of disbelief makes you more in touch with your own imagination?

_____

_____

_____

_____

_____

_____

_____

_____

_____

_____

_____

_____

_____

THE REASON I TALK TO MYSELF
IS BECAUSE I'M THE ONLY ONE
WHOSE ANSWERS I ACCEPT.

—George Carlin

Your Own
Best Audience

When have you followed someone's advice against your gut? How could listening to your own advice be helpful to you?

_____

_____

_____

_____

_____

_____

_____

_____

_____

_____

_____

_____

_____

_____

_____

Trying to be anti-cool is just one exponent of trying to be cool—it's the same beast.

—David Foster Wallace

Try Hard

Working hard to stand out or working hard to fit in are mostly just this: *exhausting*. Personalities are pendulums, never one thing that's always cool or another that's always outsider. Let yourself swing back and forth in a way that's natural for you.

WHAT FEELS GOOD ABOUT BOTH SIDES?

_____

_____

_____

_____

_____

_____

_____

_____

_____

_____

_____

LOVE YOUR FLAWS. OWN YOUR QUIRKS. AND KNOW THAT YOU ARE JUST AS PERFECT AS ANYONE ELSE, EXACTLY AS YOU ARE.

–Ariana Grande

You're a Vision

One person's nasty scar is another's ruggedly beautiful. See yourself from the lens of someone who loves your quirks wholeheartedly. What do you see?

_____

_____

_____

_____

_____

_____

_____

_____

_____

_____

_____

_____

_____

_____

One of the basic rules of the universe is that nothing is perfect. Perfection simply doesn't exist. . . without imperfection, neither you nor I would exist.

–Stephen Hawking

We Are All Stardust

Or whatever people say. If a star can explode and create galaxies, planets, human beings, and—by extension—TikTok, then your happy accidents have a purpose somewhere. What imperfections do you admire in yourself and others?

_____

_____

_____

_____

_____

_____

_____

_____

_____

_____

_____

_____

IF I'M AT A PARTY WHERE
I'M NOT ENJOYING MYSELF,
I WILL PUT SOME COOKIES IN
MY JACKET POCKET AND LEAVE
WITHOUT SAYING GOODBYE.

—Mindy Kaling, *Is Everyone Hanging Out Without Me?*

Take the Cookies and Run

Sometimes you have to go to events you don't feel like going to, like, say, your job for the rest of your life. But you are allowed to shift your perspective on social obligations. Let's call them *social suggestions*, and they have a fire exit. When could you give yourself a little slack and say no?

_____

_____

_____

_____

_____

_____

_____

_____

_____

_____

_____

You take it down a
notch. You're not the
boss of my notches.

Big Energy

Kick it up a notch. When has someone tried to kill your vibe? When have you been proud of yourself for just being you and how can you find ways to ignore those vibe killers in the future?

_____

_____

_____

_____

_____

_____

_____

_____

_____

_____

_____

_____

_____

_____

FOLLOW YOUR INNER MOONLIGHT;
DON'T HIDE THE MADNESS.

—Allen Ginsberg

Howl at the Moon

Very few people do this any more. It's too risky. First of all, it's a hell of a responsibility to be yourself. It's much easier to be somebody else or nobody at all.

—Sylvia Plath, *The Unabridged Journals of Sylvia Plath*

The Road Less Traveled.

It could be full of potholes and troll tolls, or it could be scenic and just what you need. When have you felt compelled to be like other people or melt into the background? What is it about taking your own route that feels intimidating or, alternatively, that feels like an opportunity?

_____

_____

_____

_____

_____

_____

_____

_____

_____

_____

_____

I HAVE NO TRAJECTORY.
IF I HAD A TRAJECTORY, I
PROBABLY WOULD NEVER
HAVE BEEN ABLE TO DO ALL
THE FUN THINGS I'VE DONE.

—Jameela Jamil

Ditch the
Flight Path

Leave some room for the unexpected. When have you felt restricted to a certain plan? What about relinquishing it entirely could feel freeing?

_____

_____

_____

_____

_____

_____

_____

_____

_____

_____

_____

_____

_____

_____

_____

They searched for blue
Their whole life through,
Then passed right by—
And never knew.

—Shel Silverstein, "Masks"

Eyes Open!

Find your people. No one should endure unhealthy relationships or friendships that feel like the wrong-sized shirt. When you spend all that time adjusting the fit or trying to feel good in something that feels bad, you miss the ones who are right in front of you. What do you want in a friend?

_____

_____

_____

_____

_____

_____

_____

_____

ALL i HAVE TO DO iS
SHOW UP AND ENJOY
THE MESSY, iMPERFECT,
AND BEAUTIFUL
JOURNEY OF MY LiFE.

-Kerry Washington

What a Mess!

Truly, a compliment. What may seem like chaos to someone else is that unbeatable bliss to you. What do others interpret as messy about you that you love?

_____

_____

_____

_____

_____

_____

_____

_____

_____

_____

_____

_____

I contain multitudes, most of them flawed.

—Colson Whitehead, *The Noble Hustle*

It's Called
Nuance

Even the brightest diamonds have speckles and cracks. This added detail is the special depth that makes them unique. What do you see that no one else does?

＊
+
_____

_____

_____

_____

_____

_____

_____

_____

_____

_____

_____

＊

_____

_____

_____

IF I HAD A PENNY FOR EVERY STRANGE LOOK I'VE GOTTEN FROM STRANGERS ON THE STREET, I'D HAVE ABOUT 10 TO 15 DOLLARS, WHICH IS A LOT WHEN YOU'RE DEALING WITH PENNIES.

—Andy Samberg

Cha-Ching

Make a list of the most absurd things you've ever done that gained a reaction. Do you embrace or recoil from those responses? How much weirdness cash are you gaining?

_____

_____

_____

_____

_____

_____

_____

_____

_____

_____

_____

_____

_____

_____

_____

There are no rules.
Just follow your heart.

No Rules, Just Heart

Cherish your independence. How do you want to wield it?

_____

_____

_____

_____

_____

_____

_____

_____

_____

_____

_____

_____

_____

_____

HATING THE COOL KIDS
TAKES AN AWFUL LOT OF
ENERGY, AND I'D GIVEN UP
ON IT A LONG TIME AGO.

–John Green, *Looking for Alaska*

Be the Breeze, Baby

Letting go is a lot easier than digging into your frustration. When do you find yourself stewing about people who make you feel less than? Whether it's counting to ten or imagining where you'll be in a few years' time, come up with a way to let their hot air blow past you rather than knock you down.

_____

_____

_____

_____

_____

_____

_____

_____

_____

_____

_____

_____

I am big enough to admit that I am often inspired by myself.

—Leslie Knope, Parks and Recreation

Here for the Inspo

Big ups for your brilliance! Give yourself a little credit. What about you is *that* fantastic? When have you given yourself goosebumps?

_____

_____

_____

_____

_____

_____

_____

_____

_____

_____

_____

_____

_____

WHERE THERE IS PERFECTION
THERE IS NO STORY TO TELL.

—Ben Okri

Story Time

Let's write one! You're the main character and two things go wrong. Where does this string of imagination take you?

_____

_____

_____

_____

_____

_____

_____

_____

_____

_____

_____

_____

_____

_____

_____

_____

I'm chasing
the wonder
I unravel myself
All in slow motion

—Aurora, "The Seed"

Wondrous Unraveling

_____
_____
_____
_____
_____

HOW DID IT FEEL?

_____
_____
_____
_____
_____
_____

I'M INTERESTING.
YOU TALK ABOUT ME.

—Josh, *Please Like Me*

Let Them Spill Tea.

Having a unique sparkle could mean there's a trail of whispers as you glide on by. What grand entrances have you made? What feels good about being noticed?

_____

_____

_____

_____

_____

_____

_____

_____

_____

_____

_____

_____

_____

_____

_____

Until you're ready
to look foolish,
you'll never have
the possibility of
being great.

−Cher

Be a Little Extra

There's no other way to be extraordinary. And with that comes the responsibility of letting yourself act like an idiot. What activities or new experiences can you dive into that might make you feel foolish? What good can from stepping outside your comfort zone?

_____

_____

_____

_____

_____

_____

_____

_____

_____

_____

_____

_____

_____

_____

BEING SILLY IS
STILL ALLOWED,
NOT EXCLUDED
BY ADULTHOOD.
WHAT'S EXCLUDED
BY ADULTHOOD IS
THOUGHTLESSNESS,
SO BE THOUGHTFUL
AND SILLY.

—Hank Green

Make Silliness a Practice

Okay, you'll start right now! Try to say these words in a grumpy voice: sizzle, floppy, sparkles, elephant, tickles, bubbles.

WHAT ELSE FEELS SILLY BUT GOOD?

_____

_____

_____

_____

_____

_____

_____

_____

_____

_____

_____

_____

I am not an angel, I asserted; and I will not be one till I die: I will be myself.

—Charlotte Brontë, *Jane Eyre*

stay salty

It's okay not to be a model of virtue, a rule follower, or an angel all the time. What rules do you like to break (that won't result in a night in the clink)?

_____

_____

_____

_____

_____

_____

_____

_____

_____

_____

_____

_____

_____

_____

WHERE'S YOUR WILL
TO BE WEIRD?

–Jim Morrison

Summon the Strange

What's the weirdest thing you've never done but would love to do?
Imagine a space where social consequences are of no concern.
What will you do?

_____

_____

_____

_____

_____

_____

_____

_____

_____

_____

_____

_____

When I get sad,
I stop being sad and
be awesome instead.

-Barney Stinson, *How I Met Your Mother*

You're So Awesome!

Be your awesome self. What makes you feel amped to be you?

_____

_____

_____

_____

_____

_____

_____

_____

_____

_____

_____

_____

_____

_____

_____

MAKE GLORIOUS AND
FANTASTIC MISTAKES.

WHOOPS!

—Neil Gaiman, *Make Good Art*

Failure!

It's good for you. Crash and burn in a way that dazzles.

_____
_____
_____
_____
_____
_____

_____
_____
_____
_____
_____
_____
_____
_____
_____

You may think
I'm small, but I
have a universe
inside my mind.

—Yoko Ono

Galaxies
Close to Home

What peculiarities are you hiding inside your own little universe?
How do others underestimate you when you know you have so
much to give?

_____

_____

_____

_____

_____

_____

_____

_____

_____

_____

_____

_____

_____

_____

LIKE PRECIOUS STONES,
WE HAVE A FEW FLAWS,
BUT WHY FOCUS ON THAT?
FOCUS ON WHAT YOU LIKE
ABOUT YOURSELF, AND
THAT WILL BRING YOU
HAPPINESS AND PEACE.

—Richard Simmons

I Like Me

Remind yourself what you like most about yourself. What makes you feel a peacefulness in who you are?

_____

_____

_____

_____

_____

_____

_____

_____

_____

_____

_____

_____

_____

_____

The word
"silly" derives
from the Greek
"selig" meaning
"blessed".
There is
something
sacred in
being able to
be silly.

–Paul Pearsall

#silly

Choose silliness, choose joy, choose to feel fortunate that dumb things are allowed in our every days. What kind of silliness do you sometimes take for granted? What in your life could use a little more?

_____

_____

_____

_____

_____

_____

_____

_____

_____

_____

_____

_____

_____

_____

_____

VISIONS ARE
WORTH FIGHTING FOR.
WHY SPEND YOUR LIFE
MAKING SOMEONE
ELSE'S DREAMS?

-Tim Burton

Dream a Little Dream

Put your money where your dreams are. Which of your dreams seem bananas to the people around you? What dreams do you want to follow?

_____

_____

_____

_____

_____

_____

_____

_____

_____

_____

_____

_____

I know who I was when I got up this morning, but I think I must have been changed several times since then.

−Lewis Carroll,
Alice's Adventures in Wonderland

Metamorphosis

Change is good, whether it's in the seasons or in changing your mind. How have you watched yourself change over time? What did you think was weird about yourself long ago that feels good now?

_____

_____

_____

_____

_____

_____

_____

_____

_____

_____

_____

_____

_____

_____

THAT'S WHY I THINK MY LIFE
TURNED OUT AS GOOD AS IT
HAS. BECAUSE ALL THE TIME,
I'M JUST TRYING TO HAVE FUN.

–Tiffany Haddish,
The Last Black Unicorn

Just for Funsies!

Let's not overthink it. When do you let yourself have the most fun? What makes those moments beautiful?

_____

_____

_____

_____

_____

_____

_____

_____

_____

_____

_____

_____

_____

_____

If silly things were not done, intelligent things would never happen.

—Tom Peters

Intelligence for Dummies

Brilliance comes in all forms and disguises. When have you discounted your own ideas or someone else's because they seemed too far-fetched? How could you have made space for the peculiar?

_____

_____

_____

_____

_____

_____

_____

_____

_____

_____

_____

_____

I LIKE TO THINK
WE'RE ALL THE
SUM OF OUR
EXPERIENCES, SO
NO ONE HAS MY
PERSPECTIVE.

—Ronny Chieng,
The Sydney Morning Herald

1 + 1 = You.

Cuuuute. Add up all your fun qualities, freaky tendences, funny moments, and even disasters, and you have a life chock-full of unique perspective.

HOW DO YOU SEE THINGS DIFFERENTLY?

_____

_____

_____

_____

_____

_____

_____

_____

_____

_____

_____

_____

_____

I guess I'm a little weird. I like to talk to trees and animals. That's okay though; I have more fun than most people.

—Bob Ross

Leader of the Weirds

_____

_____

_____

_____

_____

WHAT DO YOU ADMIRE ABOUT THEM?

_____

_____

_____

_____

_____

IMPERFECTIONS ARE NOT INADEQUACIES; THEY ARE REMINDERS THAT WE'RE ALL IN THIS TOGETHER.

−Brené Brown

More Than Adequate!

What has made you feel inadequate when you didn't deserve to? In what ways could you have given yourself, or been given, more credit?

_____

_____

_____

_____

_____

_____

_____

_____

_____

_____

_____

_____

_____

_____

If you've got it, flaunt it. And if you don't got it? Flaunt it. 'Cause what are we even doing here if we're not flaunting it?

–Mindy Kaling, Why Not Me?

Sashay Away

_____

_____

_____

_____

_____

_____

EMBRACE THE QUALITIES THAT MAKE YOU SPECIAL.
HOW CAN YOU SHARE THEM WITH OTHERS?

_____

_____

_____

_____

_____

_____

EVERY PERSON ON THIS EARTH
NEEDS JUST ONE PERSON WHO SEES
THEM AND ROOTS FOR THEM . . .
THE MORE THE MERRIER BUT
LET'S START WITH ONE.

—Selma Blair, *Mean Baby*

#1 Fan.

It's not always easy to tell who's in your corner. Whether big gestures or small, who has supported you or backed you up when you needed it?

_____

_____

_____

_____

_____

_____

_____

_____

_____

_____

_____

_____

_____

_____

_____

_____

_____

There's power
in looking
silly and not
caring that
you do.

−Amy Poehler

Power Up

What makes you feel powerful? Toy with matching your strength with a willingness to let go of control. What happens when you submit to your inner light?

_____

_____

_____

_____

_____

_____

_____

_____

_____

_____

_____

_____

_____

_____

_____

_____

IF I COULD GO BACK IN TIME AND SLAP ALL OF THE IDIOCY OUT OF MY MOUTH, I WOULD BE A BUSY TIME TRAVELER.

—Issa Rae, *The Misadventures of Awkward Black Girl*

Rewind!

Nothing like good ol' word vomit! When have you said cringe-worthy things that you wanted to take back? What positive spin can you put on that moment? If you can't, how would you change it?

_____

_____

_____

_____

_____

_____

_____

_____

_____

_____

_____

_____

_____

_____

And those who were
seen dancing were
thought to be insane
by those who could
not hear the music.

—Friedrich Nietzsche

Your Own Drummer

Maybe you're on another wavelength, or maybe you just love the slow R&B rhythm of your dishwasher. What's your version of dancing to a tune no one else stops to hear?

_____

_____

_____

_____

_____

_____

_____

_____

_____

_____

_____

_____

_____

_____

A FRIEND IS
SOMEONE TO
SHARE THE LAST
COOKIE WITH.

—Cookie Monster, *Sesame Street*

Sharing Is Caring

How do you share your flawsomeness with the people around you? What feels good about being wonderfully wonky with someone else?

_____

_____

_____

_____

_____

_____

_____

_____

_____

_____

_____

_____

_____

_____

POBODY'S NERFECT

Nerfection.

Get a little goofy with it. When you miss the mark, when you get tongue-tied, or when things just get all jumbly—find the fun. What's a fun way to rebound when things aren't nerfect?

_____

_____

_____

_____

_____

_____

_____

_____

_____

_____

_____

_____

_____

We're all a little weird and life's a little weird. And when we find someone whose weirdness is compatible with ours, we join up with them and fall in mutual weirdness and call it love.

-Dr. Seuss

Love You, Weirdo

WHO'S YOUR FAVORITE WEIRDO?

_____
_____
_____
_____
_____
_____
_____

WHAT MAKES THEIR WEIRD DIFFERENT FROM YOURS?

_____
_____
_____
_____
_____
_____
_____

Who you are
authentically
is alright.

YOU ARE AWESOME!

—Laverne Cox

Be Genuinely You

What makes you feel the most comfortable in your own skin? What good nods, positive vibes, or super support would feel validating? Wave your fantastically, beautifully, wonderfully flawsome ways all around you.

_____

_____

_____

_____

_____

_____

_____

_____

_____

_____

_____

_____

_____

LET YOUR
FLAWSOME
BLOSSOM